'ON THE BUSES' WITH DOSTOYEVSKY

For Mandy

GEOFF HATTERSLEY

All the Best

Geoff Hattersley 11/6/01

'ON THE BUSES'
<u>WITH</u> DOSTOYEVSKY

BLOODAXE BOOKS

ISBN: 1 85224 439 9

First published 1998 by
Bloodaxe Books Ltd,
P.O. Box 1SN,
Newcastle upon Tyne NE99 1SN.

Bloodaxe Books Ltd acknowledges
the financial assistance of Northern Arts.

Cover printing by J. Thomson Colour Printers Ltd, Glasgow.

Printed in Great Britain by
Cromwell Press Ltd, Trowbridge, Wiltshire.

For Jeanette Hattersley,
my family and friends

Acknowledgements

Acknowledgements are due to the editors of the following publications in which some of these poems, or earlier versions of them, first appeared: *Ambit, Braquemard, Dog, Draft #2* & *Final Draft* (Albert Poets anthologies), *Headlock, The North, The Penniless Press, Poetry Wales, Scratch, Verse, The Wide Skirt* and *The Yellow Crane*.

Contents

III

I

The New Mr Barnsley Something

on the front page of the *Chronicle*
once promised to crack my skull
but that's beer down the urinal

and I can turn to page two
as calmly and as amused
by his pectorals as anyone else

recalling also one Saturday night
as part of a large crowd watching
Mr Barnsley Something bouncing

another man's head on a car bonnet
while shouting 'I'll teach thee
to make eyes at our lass.'

And suddenly I wonder
what became of him –
the other man,

the one they lifted
like a ticking bomb
and drove away, slowly.

Scared

She's scared of wanting books
in tidy piles, of making sure
everything's in its proper place;

she's sure the same desire
was behind the skyscraper
supplanting the teepee

and is why maps on walls
have flags sticking in them
which uniformed men discuss.

Most days she goes nowhere,
just sort of potters round
trying not to notice

everything out of place.
She listens to the great masters,
she can talk to the cat

or hit the gin and write
letters to her only sister
who died some years ago.

Stop

'I have to spend the rest of my life with this fool,'
the woman said, jabbing her thumb at a man

wearing stained overalls and carrying
a welding helmet. I took no notice,

hoped the bus would come soon. I was on my way home
after some months of clandestine research

in the sort of place criminals would plan
a necessary assassination.

'I'm stuck with it now, God I'm stuck with it alright,
stuck with it whether I want him or don't.'

People went in and out of the bank opposite.
I felt stupid looking at them, looked at the ground.

I knew what to expect when I made my report.
I was naming names, they wouldn't like it.

What they liked wasn't my concern, but what they'd do.
They'd had things their own way for a long time.

All of a sudden I realised
I was facing downhill and not uphill.

The bus came and the couple made no move.
The man spoke for the first time: 'We don't want this one.'

It meant I was at the front of the queue, in fact
was the queue. I made it to the back seat, slid down

as far as I could, my knees high
on the back of the seat in front. I thought

of Robert Ford taking the time to aim
and a hundred other sneaky bastards

and didn't even breathe. The man threw the helmet
at the woman's feet as the bus pulled out.

Nervous Before Breakfast

A leafless tree, catprints in snow
And he doesn't notice, stone-faced always

Spraying anti-freeze all over his car
Every morning, as he gets in it, an alarm blares

You crush whatever's in your hand
You're beginning to think and act like him yourself

Leaving rubbish where you know it'll annoy him
Slamming doors at half-five in the morning

Raised voices, breaking glass, a normal day

'In our experience, the murderer
is often the last person to see the victim alive'

You turn the radio off. There's nothing else to turn on

Poem for Billy

His wife's thrown him out
again, this time
for going to Cleethorpes
for the weekend. He'd gone

Friday, instead of work –
meant to get back
early evening, ended up
too drunk. He'd phoned

to say he was still at work,
the car wouldn't start
and it might take a while
to get it fixed, it looked like a –

'What's that noise?' she'd said.
'What noise Luv?' 'Tha knows
what fuckin' noise,' she'd said,
'them fuckin' seagulls bastard.'

He opens another can of John Smith's.
'So ah stayed till Sunday neet.
Might us well gerrung
fer nickin' a sheep us a tha knows what.'

A Huge Bag of Potatoes

A huge bag of potatoes
is carried home by a woman
past a row of houses
where men are swearing
as they take the football results
from the BBC teleprinter.
The woman holds the bag
close to her body with both arms.
She's tired, looking forward
to sprucing up in a cool bathroom.

The sun's in now, but earlier
the men sat supping pints
on the steps of the Clothier's Arms,
down to their vests or bare-chested;
men with muscular arms
and beer-bellies, tattoos
and reddening flesh, moustaches
and stubble. The woman
passed them then, and they
stared after her backside.

Now she reaches her house
and puts the bag down,
feels in her pocket.
As she produces her keys, the door
opens, and a muscular, tattooed arm
picks up the bag
like a rabbit by the ears
and takes it inside.
The woman follows
and the door closes.

Norman's Tea Party

He comes in with his tray
and black armband,
injects himself in the eye,
starts whistling
'They Smoked My Cigars
But Were Good Enough
to Leave the Ash',
then hangs upside-down
from the light-fitting
and pours out the cups,
snarling the whole time.
Tiny headless animals
fall from his pockets,
also, a bag of
blood-stained broken glass.
When he's finished,
he sorts out a few bones
that he gnaws in the corner,
sitting on his heels.

Meaningless Incident

He slumps down
in the seat next to us,

blood dripping
from a large gash

near the knuckles
of his right hand,

staining his jeans.
He wraps a cloth

round the wound,
picks up his pint,

smiles at Jeanette
as he takes

one of my cigarettes,
asks if I'd like

a game of pool.
The word LEGEND

in purple ink
on his forehead.

Builder

One day he'll get the help
he needs – till then
we'll just have to put up
with him, marching
up and down the street
with his tape measures,
hammer and saw, lumps of wood.
Last week he built a fence
all round Mrs Barton's –
we could just make out
the top of her head,
hear her frail cries...

'Mornin' ter yer,'
he says to me;
he's knocking a steel post
into my front doorstep;
'nearly done, nearly done'.

Bosses

Every morning
I open the back door
to get a chestful
of fresh air, the cat
strolls in
and I feed it. Today
someone's freezing
up a telegraph pole,
a group of bosses
smirking at the foot,
discussing the next step.
I stand in the doorway
while the kettle boils
in this run-down
South Yorkshire pit village
that has no pit,
that has no theatre,
that has no crowds of tourists
photographing gardens,
that has no path leading
to a bookshop. I stand
and listen to the bosses talk.

On the Buses with Dostoyevsky

Because of the steelworks
that deafened my dad
our telly was always
too loud, so loud
it formed a second narrative
to what I was reading
up in my room
in my late teens – I'd have
Hemingway and *Kojak*,
Alias Smith and Jones and Poe.
All that noise! Car chases
and gunshots, sirens, screams,
horse racing and boxing,
adverts for fishfingers,
floor cleaner and fresh breath;
and Knut Hamsun starving,
Ahab chasing his whale.
I felt like a learner driver
stalled at a traffic light,
a line of lorries behind me.
Because of the steelworks
that closed in 1970
and which I never saw
except as a skeleton,
I like silence and calm,
I like silence and smoke
cigarettes in the dark.

Acquaintance

He's turned bitter and serious,
the fear of death
muddling up his conversation.

It's no laughing matter.
It's as if irony
was just something he grew out of.
He can't look forward
to a death bed,
has no famous last words.

He annoys me, I don't like him
sitting across from me
while I'm eating biscuits.
I don't like him
telling my jokes, claiming they're his,
expecting me to laugh.

I could pass the biscuits
and he wouldn't thank me.
I could choke and he wouldn't move.

Bravo

They've got a cheap mortgage
on a two bedroom end terrace
and have stolen some land
adjoining the property
to make a drive
for their silver Bravo.
They're building a dream home,
it's the only thing they're able
to talk about.
They go in carrying pieces,
are trying hard.
They've never stopped,
and their youthful faces
can't hide the mounting excitement –
before too long they'll be ready
to sell, buy
that three bedroom semi-detached
on the street where no one will think
anything different to them.
They're keen to get away
from ruffians
who play music too loud,
too loud being at all.

'It's dead simple,' says Mark,
'I'm phoning the police.'
'Yes Mark,' says Jean, 'phone them.'
Mark phones the police; the police
laugh their socks off
when they get there.

Grace

died in a hospital bed
surrounded by her family.
She'd been unconscious
days on end
then suddenly sat up and
looked her husband
right in the eye.
They were both
eighty-three.

I sat there
a while, just her and me.
I wanted to believe
somehow, somewhere, something
of her still lived.
I held her hand
and thought about a dream
I'd had when I was four.
Grace saved me from a lion,
beating it off with a poker
at the top of the cellar steps.

Numbered

Dirty buses, always crowded.
The sign above the shop says FLOREST.
Bottles and chip papers
piling up at the curb, a young girl
with the blankest face
pushing a beat-up pram –
I'd take off if I could,
just leap into the air
and glide away over the church steeple.

Last night a distressing experience.
While crunching toast
a lower back tooth broke in half.
It doesn't hurt but it doesn't seem right
not to do anything about it.

I tell someone at the workshop
that the days of the community newspaper
are numbered.
The days of the community
are numbered, he replies.

High on my list of necessities
is a warm room where I can hear
the sound of people going places,
the clacking of high heels
as I trawl through old books and pamphlets
for the one true classic
I've forgotten all about
that will bring joy into my life.

Her Place

Her fridge wasn't working
and a bucket of water
in the corner of her room
was stuffed with bottles of lager
and cheap white wine
while she danced with her eyes closed
in this bent-kneed way she had
to the jazz station
her radio stayed tuned in to.
I stood in the doorway
grinning, with a cigarette,
not sure if she knew I was there or not.
Then she smelled the smoke,
opened her eyes and saw me.

She'd attempted suicide
half a dozen times
and complained constantly
of headache, toothache, backache,
and that she needed a man.
She walked with a theatrical limp.
'Darling,' she'd say, 'I am in such pain today.'
Everyone was 'Darling',
male or female,
and she was always in pain.
I used to go to her place once a month
to buy tobacco.
She knew a lorry driver
and sold it cheap.

Date

He checks his hair
in the mirror
and his teeth
being a cause for concern
rehearses
a different smile.

His wife lives on
in his parrot
squawking
Put that guitar down
till you bloody
learn to play it.

II VOLUNTEER

For Joe and Jaffa Dana

Holy Air

I

This is where Jesus gave his life.
It's illegal to drive a bus unarmed
and the drivers wear side-holsters,
strut round the station like a posse.
A dozen soldiers share the seats with you,
nursing their rifles, never letting go.

This is where Jesus gave his life
and the bazaars are full of it.
You need money, a lot,
and Arabs will follow you down the street –
'I can sell you a jar of Holy Air
at a reasonable price.'

II

'This street is closed,'
says a young Arab boy
suddenly blocking my path,
'bad Muslims.'
He holds out his hand
and I give him a shequel
as the call to prayer
rolls across the rooftops.
God is great! he shouted
as he detonated the bomb
strapped to his chest.
Something like this happens
and does not stop.

Not for Aesthetic

I'm to work with Mario,
an Argentinian carpenter
who's been on the kibbutz
six years. He arrives
on a bicycle, a white Labrador
trailing behind. With winter
peeping round the corner,
it's important we paint
the outside of some new
wooden buildings. 'Not
for aesthetic, but to…'
He blinks behind his glasses
and waves his hands,
his English failing him.
'Protect,' I say.
'Yes,' he says.
Today though the sun is hot
and I take off my shirt,
can feel my back roasting
as I slap grey paint
unceremoniously.
It's hard to believe
it's November; back home
they'll be buttoning big coats,
wrapping their scarves.
But Mario insists
that here too it will be cold
and raining before long.
He constantly apologises
for his English:
'I study it five years
two hours each week
but I never speak it.'
Really I have no trouble
understanding him, though
he doesn't seem to get
much of what *I* say.

'It's my northern accent,'
I tell him, 'we're poor
and can't speak properly.'
'In Argentina, the south
poor and the north…'
'Prosperous.'
'Yes.' And later,
the work done, walking home,
Mario pushing his bicycle
and the dog trotting
alongside, nosing the grass
for lizards or hedgehogs,
I try to tell him more
about the north of England –
the pits shut, the unemployment,
Thatcher's legacy.
'In my country,' he says,
'we call the Malvinas
Thatcher's war.'
The dog runs barking
to the foot of a tree.
'In mine too,' I reply
in my clearest English.
He nods, and shouts something
at the now frantic dog.

November

The young Israelis
accept their lot.
Here at this kibbutz breakfast table
are a dozen, boys and girls
who'll soon be soldiers.
And the long hair of the boys,
hanging over the backs
of their Jim Morrison
and Nirvana t-shirts,
or tied in ponytails,
and the rings through the noses
of the girls and some boys,
will go, must go, in March.
November, they sit
cheerfully eating eggs
and reading their newspapers
back to front, left to right:
five soldiers wounded slightly
near the Lebanese border;
one killed in a drive-by shooting
in the quiet town of Safad;
three killed, one left paralysed
by a suicide bomber
at Netzarim junction.
This is the daily news.
And I sit with them
and chew toast and jam,
thirty-eight and British
and safe, and wonder if
any will make the news
themselves?

Volunteer

You're not sure if it's Monday or Wednesday –
you're working eight hours a day, six days a week;
you don't have a television
or anything happening socially
to distinguish the days.
You can forget who you are,
what you are, back home, all that.
You've done your shift in the kitchen;
your shoes are split from standing in water;
now you cherish the hot earth
beneath your bare feet
as you sit nursing a beer
while your skin darkens.
You can pick up the *Jerusalem Post*,
squinting in the sun as you read
'the rabbi was shot several times in the head and face and lost
        control of his car.'
You can put it back down.
You can play backgammon
with a South African who says
'Do you mind if I'm white? I wouldn't want to be black.'
Which makes it a pleasure
to beat him.

Town

There's always a saxophone
in the background of a scene like this
or at least a trumpet.
Which doesn't make it any less real,
but as you approach the building
you're hearing a soundtrack
that exists only in your head.
Rain gathers in large holes,
making you hop along the pavement,
while taxi-drivers give rough rides,
leaning over the back seat saying
'They ought to get off their butts.'
You can't go in a lot of these places
without being questioned briefly,
perhaps searched for guns or explosives.
But the saxophone helps you through it
though there are no saxophones here.

Piper

At the age of thirty-seven
he owns only what he stands in
and enough stuff to fill a duffel bag
but he's not worried.
He stopped worrying about the future
the day he left Germany
to avoid the draft,
losing himself in Amsterdam
with a woman who could keep up.
He made a living.
The day the police arrested him
he had a ticket to see Dylan –
for more than one decade
this had been an ambition.
Instead, he got to spend two years
reading Albert Camus and Herman Hesse,
Charles Bukowski and Jack Kerouac.
It was like being back
in the orphanage.

Pale and skinny, hardly
a word to say for himself.
We see him quickly change
into a muscular, tanned raconteur,
holding court on his porch
all afternoon and evening
until something, the past
or some version of the future,
puts a bottle of vodka
firmly in his hand
and clouds his eyes.
And he's turning up for work drunk,
seven in the morning.

A Week

They pose for photos
with leggy blondes, the young soldiers,
will even let them stroke their rifles –
this within a hundred metres
of the Wailing Wall,
where the black-suited, bobbing hassidim
chant their prayers.
Only because of the soldiers
are the hassidim safe,
and the soldiers detest them –
frisk them brusquely at checkpoints,
then shove them on with a sneer
and leave the likes of me unmolested.

A week in Jerusalem
is like the rest of your life.
Each morning in the café
just inside Jaffa Gate
I'd see the same European
sitting by the window,
already on his third or fourth beer,
rubbing bloodshot eyes
as the sun struck the silverware,
now and then jotting something
in a small notebook,
afterwards shutting it sharply
with an aggrieved sigh.

Something from a Stupor

He held a bottle of Gold Star up
and peered into it solemnly.
Told me for the tenth time
he was just 'one of the guys',
something reptilian
about the stare he fixed me with
through the green glass of the bottle.
He was young enough to be a son
I'd disown,
the sort of man who'd rip
somebody's photo to pieces.
He glanced from face
to face, grinning;
the two fat blokes at our table
left with their expensive cameras.
'We don't need them,' he said, and
laughed, 'I don't need anybody.'
Then the noise started, the disco,
and he was off and dancing,
leaving behind his untouched beer
and a smell like gunpowder.
I saw him only one more time, a glimpse,
just before the place closed
at five in the morning,
of a small group of men his own age
herding him through the door,
his cries
drowned out
by *Trenchtown Rock*.

Both Liars

They were both liars, boring as well,
though the girl falling out of the window
story was at least
energetic. The eldest
was drunk, an idiot half the time,
unconscious the rest.
'You don't like to talk to me,' he said,
vodka in my face in a bus
on the way to the Dead Sea.
'No, I like to,' I replied,
'but not at six in the morning.'
That evening I'd see him
throw a mattress round a garden
furiously, shouting
in his own language.
I'd stand and watch
for a quarter of an hour.

The young one was different,
walked in on us making love,
stood in the doorway
not three feet from the bed
and talked about a phone call
he was expecting.
Simple was not the word.
He pummelled a punchbag
suspended from a tree
for one hour each afternoon
beneath a scorching sun.
And he'd run, for one hour,
then sit staring into space
while he got his breath back
for two hours.
The day they escorted the drunk one
onto the bus, making it clear
he'd better not come back,
the punchbag one forgot
to punch his bag.
Then remembered.

The Chickens

Like a spiv
from the Second World War
he passes the chickens
through the dishwasher hatch,
turns and gets away quick
as I stuff them
in my laundry bag.

Two more hours
and the shift will be done.
I'll be in the shower,
then playing backgammon
in the afternoon sun.
The chickens defrosting.
None of us

can stomach
another kibbutz dinner –
cottage cheese, green peppers,
boiled eggs, stale bread.
The chickens down to me,
I'll sit back while the rest
do the work.

Tapping my feet
to the rhythm guitar.
The fire in the darkness,
our shapes huddled round it.
The meat sizzling, spitting.
The dogs inching closer,
told to lie down.

Massacre

I'm on my morning break,
trying to eat corn flakes
while taking the news in.
Everyone's stunned by this one:
Suicide bomber, Beit Lid junction.
Twenty-two soldiers killed,
all aged eighteen, nineteen, twenty.

Henri has the day off.
His long hair tucked under a hat,
he sits with his cigarettes
and coffee, waiting for a lift
to a school reunion
at a graveside in the city.
No one wants to talk

or risk meeting someone
who hasn't heard.
All round the room
people push their plates aside,
the food only picked at.
They go back to work early,
each with the same stooped gait.

The *Jerusalem Post* has photos
of all those who died.
They crowd pages two and three
with youthful smiles,
with eyes that do not blink,
that gaze confidently
at the future.

Dishwasher

She turns the radio
louder and lights
one of my cigarettes.
She's seventeen
and sick to death of what
we have to do.

Down on my hands and knees
scrubbing the drains
I stare at her bare feet
as she dances.
They're so brown and pretty
I almost faint.

Later, our chief tells her
she doesn't care
about her work.
'It's bad enough,' she says,
'to have to *do* this job,
do I have to care too?'

Bruise

Since I slipped
and spent fifteen minutes
on my back moaning
at the hub of a circle
of concerned and amused faces
I've had pins and needles
in my right hand. I thought
I'd broken my elbow
but it was only bruised.
The doctor gave me some painkillers
which have a real buzz,
better than the vodka – 'wodka'
it says on the bottles here.
Actually, the wodka
tastes like petrol, not that

I've ever drunk petrol.
Listen, a few minutes ago
I put down Norman's book.
It was archetypal Norman,
I mean he was just
blowing his own trumpet,
and he doesn't even have
a very good one –
he must have bought it
at Woolworth's
back in the seventies.
'What was the book like?' Jeanette asks.
'It was interesting,' I reply,
'as was having a toe amputated
when I was nineteen.'

Piper Again

He comes out at ten,
joins me on the porch.
The morning's hot;
we're in our shorts,
bare-chested, barefoot.
He can't remember
much of what happened –
he walked home about five,
the sun was coming up.
I watch his tattoos jerking
as he coughs, clutching his ribs.
Did I still have that bottle of wine,
did I think I could get it for him?
'I need it very quickly.'
By twelve it's finished
and I'm on my way to lunch;
he's not hungry,
and has managed
to get hold of
six bottles of beer.
'Bon appetit!'
he shouts after me,
over the radio.

The Barking of Stray Dogs

The barking of stray dogs
outside my window
in the middle of the night
doesn't bother me
any more, not a bit,
well maybe a bit.
So much is funny
it's hard to know where to finish –
behaving like one
of the Blues Brothers,
or spending the whole day
slicing carrots, a man of my
whatever.

Tequila is good
mixed with grapefruit,
if you've the patience
to squeeze them. Traffic passes
and is not noticed,
like the early stages
of a mental illness.
The locals' word for a hangover
is also their word
for a stray dog.

Eyad's Cassette Tape

The night before we leave
Eyad arrives from Qalqilya
to shake hands and say goodbye
and give us a cassette tape –
'good Arab music, something
to remember me with.'
I'm too drunk to talk properly
to a man who never drinks
but he's used to it
and knows I'm being stupid
when I ask if he'd like
a game of chess; he only
taught me the rules a month ago.
Eyad, who was surprised
to hear there was poverty
and despair in England too.

The afternoon at Ben Gurion
is sweaty, two security women
grilling us for thirty minutes already
when one asks if anyone
gave us anything to put in our bags?
Even as I say no
I remember the cassette tape
and just for an instant
Eyad is not a friendly,
intelligent and humane person
but just another young Muslim
who wants to kill Jews
to be sure of a place in Heaven
but whatever I think
it seems my face stays the same
because the security women
don't doubt I'm not carrying
anything suspicious.

III

Politics

It's like watching a film
of your own funeral.
You're shouting I'M ALIVE
but no one can hear you.

Across a room, two men
assess each other's silence.
They yawn and cough,
cross and uncross thin legs.

It takes years.
Ice forms on the cameras
that bring us news.
And then the men nod,

and then they rise.
One claps, then holds up a hoop
the other leaps through.
They both shout BOOM!

Home Video

Everything's still in boxes, and Jeanette
eats a boiled egg out of the centre of a toilet roll.
'Maybe we could make these for a living?' I say,
'there's always plenty of fools, they'll be queuing up

to buy toilet roll egg cups.' She dips a soldier,
I switch the radio on. I can't say what it is
but I wouldn't call it music. The tuner sticks
at the station, I can't move it... At least

the phone's connected; it rings; 'Hello?'
'It's about time I gave you a piece of my mind,'
says Norman. 'Don't make it too big a piece,'
I reply, 'or you won't have any left.'

Manuscript Discovered Behind a Bathroom Tile

I can't play guitar any more,
my fingers have got soft.
I never *could* play, but
at least I used to try.
The neighbours, true to form,
didn't like it one bit.
'If people want to live
next door to a churchmouse,'
I used to say, 'they should
move into a churchyard.'

Back then, I loved cats, loved
to have them around me.
There were ten or fourteen of them,
the only things
I didn't want to hurt.
They'd go to sleep with me, purring.
I used to imagine
drinking myself to death
and ending up half-eaten
before I was discovered.

It's true I was drinking,
working on a novel:
CONVERSATIONS WITH DISGUSTING LITTLE GEEZERS.
It was all written just like that
in upper case.
I'd get up, type a few pages,
get drunk, try to play my guitar.
Then I'd be ready
to go back to bed.

I remember the day
I made a pile of the pages
and quietly tore them;
it was winter, quite cold;
I'd had a dream the night before
that I lived in a town
where *Little House on the Prairie*

was what life was actually like.
I knew at that moment
I couldn't have a novel inside me,

that all my attempts to get serious
would always end with a chuckle.
These days I try to keep my life simple,
but sooner or later
I'm left with no choice but
to seek out a clean shirt.
If I remember to comb my hair,
I comb it. I shake my head
as I read the morning paper,
which makes my life worthwhile.

Poem Mentioning a Sweeping Brush

It was the ugliest room of the lot.
Well, they expected him to live in it.
Of course he said he'd take it, and the job,
being badly in need of a good meal.

Six months (half a year!) he did it, learning
to use a sweeping brush the proper way,
leaning on it when no one was watching.

Sometimes he'd count the change in his pocket
and try to imagine where he'd end up.
It had taken the best part of his life
to realise that not everyone

had always been wrong. Now everything
was as clear as the skin on a snare drum,
as an army marching across his tongue.

Still Grinning

The black boys on the train, three of them, in high spirits
are darting up and down the aisle,
whacking each other over the head
with rolled-up copies of discarded
Independents and *Guardians*,
their laughter filling the carriage
like a soundtrack from a shoestring movie,
and the other passengers, white mostly, over sixty,
the corners of their mouths turned down
in the way of religious fanatics
who've stumbled across a peep-show,
are looking at them like they could kill them
or put them in a cage for the rest of their lives –
the black boys oblivious
or else knowing but not giving a shit.
Their noise makes me grin for the whole journey,
till I get off at the place I've moved to,
where almost all the old whites get off too,
to board the bus that takes them into town,
that passes me when I'm halfway up the hill,
panting and still grinning.

Six Ways to Say O.K.

Church clock announcing midnight like a patriarch
It's been time to go to bed for centuries

Drunk shoes, drunk suit and tie, drunk cigarette
Eyes like a horse with its guts hanging out

Drunk key, drunk door and doormat, drunk light-switch
Drunk armchair beckoning

*

The evening was a joke I'd heard before
I swallowed something that left a bad taste

It was friendship or acted quite like it
Had to pull his fingers out of my throat

Two-faced liar harbouring a grievance
He borrowed my moustache permanently

*

My head is a vandalised slot machine
I look out from it like a hanging judge

The trick is to pretend the noise has stopped
It's not always easy

A paper boat for a paper journey
See the bloated corpses in the blue pool

*

When I look at the clock I see faces
A man with a too-pretty wife sat weeping

They put the best traps where you least expect
Who the hell is 'They'? They is them and them

The breath in a party balloon knows this
A cigar knows it, and a bloody war

*

Sometimes you speak and no one takes notice
Or they mishear, call you John when you're Bob

You wipe your sweating brow on a towel
You look in the mirror: you know that guy

Sometimes you have to stand on the table
You have to shout. You have to shout louder

*

I can see the clock and what time it is
A young woman accepts a cigarette

Something worth looking at, and then the drums
I said let's go, why not? I said, let's go

Making love the couple were astonished
The loudness of midnight, then the laughter

God and Bananas

In the letter he complained of tiredness.
He was tired, he wrote, of losing at chess
and winning at chess, tired of being drunk
and not being drunk, tired of drunks talking
about god and bananas, egg-timers
and elephants. He was tired of wishing
he'd said something, then saying it; he said
he was tired most of all of being tired.

He knows this is the room where he will die,
leaving nothing to remember him by
but a brown stain on the ceiling above his bed.
He re-reads the letter about tiredness,
like someone searching for something precious
on their hands and knees and almost sobbing.

Straight

I can't trust anyone
who doesn't doubt himself some of the time.
I can always hear him,
like a radio that can't be switched off
coming through a thin wall.
I had friends but they disappeared
like smoke through an open window.
I keep ticking over, I don't know how
in this drab place
where everything gets taken for granted.
I stare at the damp patch on the ceiling,
at the hole worn in the carpet.
I say 'hello' on my doorstep
in the sun, it's not hard.
I spray weeds on the path, whistling
in an old pair of jeans.

Jupiter

I've been lost in a study of Jupiter.
Thirty-three hundred times the size of earth

but no movie industry to speak of,
hence no awards ceremonies and no

microphones in the faces of nothing.
I explained all this in the town centre

but people seemed eager to ignore me.
Ah, people. They like to think they know me

by my black moustache and curly red wig
and the wheelchair I push in front of me

containing the rag doll, ukulele,
and ghetto blaster I sing along with.

They know my favourite song is *Love Me Do*,
which I croon to a punk backing, they know

my coat for all weathers is grey cotton.
They don't know how I ache in these old bones.

They know yobbos sometimes gang up on me.
They don't know what the boots taste like.

How It Went

I

'O.K., let's do it. It won't be the first time
I've travelled in a car boot...'

He seems to be sleeping
less and less, up at four, washed and shaved
and wide awake by five – on good mornings
he feels like the first goat
able to play piano with its teeth.

The news is a series of pranks,
a schoolboyish humour he must have grown out of.

Returned from a severe haircut
and with nothing in his pocket
he smokes a cigarette that hits his chest
like a hammer. And stares through the window
at the departing summer.

II

He is a sap, he knows this for a fact,
evidence is all around him
like silly wallpaper, a bookcase full of books
he's never read, never will read.
But people traipsing round the streets
with briefcases and narrow minds?
He'd nail his tongue to the back door
rather than take part in all that.
Hungry, he opens a tin of mushy peas,
eating them cold, with a teaspoon, in the darkness.

III

He can't believe for one minute
that a man could transform
into a bird by force of will.
A pig, maybe, but not a bird, no way.
It's hard to imagine anything
less like a man than a bird –
or, come to think of it, a pig,
a friendly creature
that wishes no one harm,
content to live out its time
with its face in a trough
without ever seeking to explain it
or look beyond it.
They're the last things a man could end up as,
however hard he tried.
No amount of practice would help.

IV

He holds the newspaper up, shaking it.
'Have you heard about this?' he asks.
He replies that he hasn't, so he tells
himself all about it for the third time.

He opens the window to let some air in, some noise.
'Someone who notices nothing
suddenly notices something!'
he shouts at the astonished passers-by.

The Visit

He came over about three months ago.
He got drunk. I got drunk. My wife got drunk.
Then we put him on a train and went to bed.

He'd blathered on about so many things –
his wife, his son, his teeth, his dog, prison.
I remember it like a burning hand.

He said he wished he'd been alive
before science and mass entertainment,
before all the magic became debunked,

and knew for a fact we were all equally doomed.
He had the evidence. I sighed
when he started to produce it –

box after box, cutting after cutting
covering twenty years, twenty damn years
of downright bloody single-mindedness.

Rum and Blue Sky

It was the time of day he liked the most,
before everyone got busy.
Just the one drink, straight down, then he was out,
striding along the disused railway track,
his old dog barely able to keep up.
All those people! He had no time for them,
them or their dull regulations.
He'd had no choice in jail, they'd seen to that;
that was part of it. Well he was free now.
He reached the bridge where he always turned back;
the sky was a clear blue pressed handkerchief.
He felt the weight of the bottle, kissed it,
took a mouthful of rum and kept going.

Through it all he'd stayed true to his own dreams.
And here he was, breathing. Even his dog
seemed to hear the promise the day whispered
to soar like a frisbee thrown at the sun.
He adjusted the cardboard in his shoes.
He was humming something joyful, something
he couldn't put a name to but knew well.

The Ankles

The ankles of the woman
and the red open-toed sandals

on the stone steps as she descends
from the insurance offices –

and my head had been brimming
over with money problems!

The street full of summer,
fresh air slapping my face

like a woman trying to wake me up –
those aches in my joints, I'll ignore

them, and now
two young girls who might be sisters

cross the road with a pushchair,
their faces shining with laughter.

About Something

The life and soul of the party? Not you.
Cold as a pie in a dying man's fridge
is how you feel in these four walls. Because
it's sad, the world, and wrong-headed, a place
you're stuck in waiting for your teeth to go.

You've got the collected symphonies of
Beethoven and Mahler, you've got Mozart.
You've got something going with a woman.
But now you don't see her all that often
and you've no time to listen to music.

You feel like you're stuck between two places
and don't belong in or like either one.
You know you're passionate about something
but half the time you forget what it is
and now and then even what it isn't.

Captain Value

Disappointment at the nth interview.
What it's about, this life, is endurance.

On whose terms is he unemployable?
How will he get his rotten teeth seen to?

He changes razor blades and cuts himself,
the local paper clatters through the box,

he gets the train with the usual bunch
of old people in need of new outfits

who go looking for bargains in Barnsley.
There are plenty but they can't afford them.

Sunday Western

The new age travellers who don't travel
are zonked outside the pub in their torn clothes

and I've got a hard-on for a woman
riding a horse in the Sunday Western,

pursued by Indians down a gully.
Old films are always best, unless they're crap.

There are screwed-up beer cans strewn on our path.
They're mine, I threw them there. No one else did.